What's for Dinner?

Written by Jo Windsor

This caterpillar likes to eat leaves.

leaves

This giraffe likes
to eat leaves, too.

leaves

This cow likes
to eat grass.

grass

7

This lion likes to eat meat.

meat

This orangutan likes to eat bananas.

bananas

This boy likes to eat bananas, too.

bananas

Index

▬▬ Guide Notes

Title: What's for Dinner?

Stage: Emergent – Magenta

Genre: Nonfiction (Expository)

Approach: Guided Reading

Processes: Thinking Critically, Exploring Language, Processing Information

Written and Visual Focus: Photographs (static images), Index, Labels

Word Count: 38

FORMING THE FOUNDATION

Tell the children that this book is about different animals and insects and their food.
Talk to them about what is on the front cover. Read the title and the author.
Focus the children's attention on the index and talk about the animals that are in this book.
"Walk" through the book, focusing on the photographs and talk about the different types of food the animals and insects have and where they get it.

Read the text together.

THINKING CRITICALLY

(sample questions)

After the reading
• Why do you think the caterpillar is eating the leaf?
• How do you think the lion got the meat?

EXPLORING LANGUAGE

(ideas for selection)

Terminology
Title, cover, author, photographs

Vocabulary
Interest words: caterpillar, leaves, giraffe, cow, lion, meat, orangutan, bananas, eat
High-frequency words: this, likes, to